W9-BNS-394

picnics

DELICIOUS RECIPES FOR OUTDOOR ENTERTAINING

Sara Deseran

Photographs by Jonelle Weaver

CHRONICLE BOOKS

SAN FRANCISCO

Text copyright © 2004 by Chronicle Books LLC
Photographs copyright © 2004 by Jonelle Weaver
All rights reserved. No part of this book may be reproduced in any form without written permission from the publisher.

Library of Congress Cataloging-in-Publication Data:
Deseran, Sara.
Picnics : delicious recipes for outdoor entertaining / by Sara Deseran; photographs by Jonelle Weaver.
p. cm.
Includes index.
ISBN 0-8118-4299-1 (hardcover)
1. Outdoor cookery. 2. Picnicking. I. Title.
TX823.D473 2004
641.5'78—dc22
2003017326

Manufactured in China.
Design: Carole Goodman, Blue Anchor Design
Prop stylist: Paige Hicks
Food stylist: Liza Jernow
Assistant food stylist: Jennifer Cohen
Photographer's assistant: Teresa Horgan

Photographer Jonelle Weaver wishes to give special thanks to Paige Hicks, Liza Jernow, Jennifer Cohen, and Teresa Horgan for long hours of work; Scott and Lisa Isherwood, Kate Green, The Parker House Inn, and The Quechee Lakes Association for lovely locations; and Per Furmark for home base support.

Distributed in Canada by Raincoast Books
9050 Shaughnessy Street
Vancouver, British Columbia V6P 6E5

10 9 8 7 6 5 4 3 2 1

Chronicle Books LLC
85 Second Street
San Francisco, California 94105

www.chroniclebooks.com

Coke is a registered trademark of The Coca-Cola Co., Corona is a registered trademark of Cerveceria Modelo S.A. DE C.V., Igloo is a registered trademark of Igloo Products Corporation, Oreo is a registered trademark of Nabisco Brands Co., Pacifico is a registered trademark of Cerveceria del Pacifico, A.S. De C.V., San Pellegrino is a registered trademark of San Pellegrino S.P.A., Tabasco is a registered trademark of McIlhenny Co., Thermos is a registered trademark of King-Seeley Thermos Co., Tupperware is a registered trademark of Dart Industries, Tony Chachere's Seasoning is a registered trademark of Creole Foods, Inc. of Opelousas.

ACKNOWLEDGMENTS

Thanks to everyone that gave feedback on recipes for this book, including Alan and Jina, the 7x7 potluck team, and my husband, Colin. Thanks to Leslie and the Chronicle Books staff for calling me up, and I can never say enough to Dad, the dishwasher, and Mom, my silent partner, who developed, shopped, cooked, and tested ten variations of a peach crisp before we decided on a nectarine tart!

TABLE OF CONTENTS

INTRODUCTION

THERE'S SOMETHING ABOUT ABANDONING THE FORMALITIES OF THE dining room and taking it outdoors that just makes food taste better. Utensils are optional; so are tables and chairs. Suddenly, what matters most isn't a pressed linen tablecloth or crystal goblets, but a beautiful vista and the shade of a tree. Maybe it's the fresh air, but with the kitchen far away, appetites seem to grow even more ravenous.

One of the joys of picnicking is that there are no hard rules. The idyllic scene you see in movies (you know, the one with a wicker basket and red-and-white checked blanket laid out in a breezy meadow dotted with poppies) is just one of countless scenarios. In real life, a picnic is just as likely to be a reward at the end of a long hike, a backyard barbecue under a low-slung oak, or a romantic brown-bag lunch for two in a city park. It's a tailgate party, a beach cookout, and a playground potluck.

And there are so many good reasons to take it outside. Picnics make the most of a stunning summer day and the view of a setting sun. With no confines of a house, there's plenty of space for the kids (and the adults) to play. And from a practical standpoint, cleaning up isn't much of an issue. No dusting the house before the guests arrive, no washing a mile-high pile of dishes and silverware for hours after they depart.

WHAT TO COOK

Perhaps the hardest thing about a picnic is deciding what to make. Last minute cooking is out; you have to think about what will hold up for a couple hours out of the fridge. And unfortunately, the casual element of a picnic often lowers everyone's standards, relegating it to a spread of soda, hot dogs, and chips.

But there are plenty of ways to create a picnic that's just as memorable as your last dinner party, without making a pit stop at the mini-mart. A homemade sweet roasted pepper relish can take grilled sausages to new heights (just don't skimp on the buns). Summer berry pudding—a 20-minute endeavor—beats the biggest bag of Oreos. And if nothing else, a nice selection of cheese, fruit, cured meats, and a crusty baguette is a no-cook guarantee.

Still, sometimes it's fun to raise the bar for special occasions: a wedding anniversary calls for cold salmon, asparagus salad, and a frosty bottle of champagne (maybe even served in crystal flutes); a birthday becomes a real party with homemade coconut cupcakes. Even sandwiches don't have to be made up of deli meats and presliced cheese. Try a roasted eggplant sandwich with herbed goat cheese or even a spicy Vietnamese sandwich stuffed with a crunchy daikon and carrot slaw.

WINE, BEER, SPIRITS, AND COOLERS (AND LOTS OF WATER)

Food may be the centerpiece of a good picnic, but don't neglect the beverage choice. Although winter picnics call for a thermos of mulled cider, most picnicking is done when the summer sun is out. On sweltering days, a good refreshing drink can be the highlight of the menu.

Most importantly, think light. For beers, pilsners and ales are perfect. Icy bottles of Mexican labels, like Corona and Pacifico, are always good, especially when topped with a wedge of lime.

When choosing wines, go for easy-drinking choices such as Sauvignon Blanc, Pinot Blanc, drier Rieslings (look for those from Australia), and Pinot Grigio; these whites tend to be more food-friendly (and hot weather friendly) than the ever-popular buttery and oaky Chardonnays. Good quality rosés are also another wonderful choice. (And don't completely dismiss all reds; a Beaujolais Nouveau, slightly chilled, is another excellent option.) Unless a special occasion demands the very best champagne, there are plenty of affordable sparkling wines that will go well with everything from a sandwich to slow-roasted salmon. Look for an Italian Prosecco or a Spanish Cava. A bottle of these sprightly sparklers is reasonably priced and provides something that's both delicious and casual.

Although martinis aren't what you're looking for, mixed drinks are another option. For a picnic, it's best to go heavy on the fresh-fruit mixers and light on the spirit. Try slices of fresh pineapple stirred into pineapple juice mixed with tequila, and a splash of grenadine or an icy pitcher of fresh-squeezed lime margaritas. Sangria, made with either red or white wine, is fun. Fresh herbs add a nice twist: the mojito, a popular Cuban drink, is made with copious amounts of fragrant mint, and a few crushed leaves of lemon verbena or pineapple sage delicately add another dimension to a glass of sparkling wine.

Virgin coolers are a wonderful alternative to the usual Igloo full of Coke. Offer things like fresh lemonade with ginger and honey or iced tea made with any number of teas (both herbal and black) or mixed with cranberry or hibiscus juice. Mexican-inspired *aguas frescas* made with purées of fresh fruit such as watermelon, cantaloupe, or mango are also wonderful.

And last, but not least, don't forget the water—still water (sparkling waters often have sodium in them). Keep a cooler full of bottled water or a pitcher or two out on the table. You don't want your guests to get dehydrated.

PACK IT UP

Once you've got your picnic fare prepared, it's time to get it ready to go. A good selection of airtight plastic containers is essential to have on hand. Not only do they keep things fresh, they keep more delicate items like vegetables and fruit from getting crushed. Tiny containers are perfect for storing salad dressings until it's time to dress the salad, and will keep a handful of sliced almonds crisp until you're ready to scatter them over the green beans. Long, flat containers work well for transporting skewered meats, prepped to throw on the grill. And there's no need to transfer a salad from a plastic container to a proper serving bowl once you arrive at the picnic. Tupperware and other brands now make attractive bowls that are meant to serve both purposes; just remove the top and use the same container to serve.

Of course, certain things can be toted in heavy-duty lock-top plastic bags. This often works well for marinating meats. As for sandwiches? Plastic wrap is fine, but the moisture it traps inside can make crusty breads, such as a baguette, get soft. If you want to maintain the bread's integrity, take a note from your local deli and wrap the sandwiches in something like thin butcher paper or even parchment paper.

Once you've got your food prepared, pack it up: from wicker baskets complete with matching real china and silverware to insulated backpacks and wine bottle totes to monster SUV-style coolers that practically have four-wheel drive, as well as umbrellas, canopies, and tents—there's no shortage of options for serious picnicking. In fact, there are shops and Web sites devoted to it. Although your choices are endless, when purchasing your picnic carriers, make sure to consider what kind of picnicking you plan to do. If you hike, a backpack makes sense (there are those that hold enough for a party of two or a party of four). If you do a lot of big beach barbecues, you might consider a large hard-topped cooler. And if you're just walking from your apartment to the city park, consider a soft, collapsible cooler with a shoulder strap. If none of this is in your budget, or you only picnic on occasion, any plain old, non-insulated backpack or a big farmers' market–style basket—both packed with lock-top plastic bags and ice packs—should do you just fine.

DRESS IT UP

They might not be four star style, but tableware choices are endless, too. For a little fiesta, try setting a Mexican-inspired picnic table with a bright, floral-patterned oil cloth that can be wiped down with ease. Inexpensive woven mats, available at most import stores, are perfect for rolling out on either sand or lawn and tend to stay drier than a blanket. If nothing else, just throw down a tarp to avoid getting wet grass stains on your grandmother's quilt. For a more comfortable picnic, one item that's worth investing in is a lightweight folding chair made of canvas and aluminum. They even come with their own shoulder-bag carriers.

When it comes to setting the table, a large party almost requires sturdy paper plates, but for a smaller party, invest in some unbreakable acrylic. Much sturdier than cheaper plastic, acrylic picnic ware comes in all sorts of stylish shapes and colors, in everything from glasses to plates and bowls. And best of all, it can be used again and again with no waste.

Although the whole point of a picnic is to keep it simple, there's nothing wrong with adding a little something to set the mood. For a twilight picnic, candles—citronella candles in particular—add a flicker of light and keep the mosquitoes at bay. Paper Chinese lanterns—even with no lights in them—look festive strung between trees and a few sprays of freshly picked wildflowers add a little cheer. And if you're setting up camp in a park, it's a good idea to display a little wind sock or some satin streamers to help your guests find your location.

PICNIC FOOD SAFETY

Of course, being outdoors means dealing with the elements that come with it. And when it comes to food safety, the sun is your enemy. When transporting and serving food outdoors, remember that it needs some special treatment. Here are some basic rules to follow:

Packing for the Picnic

- Chill all food thoroughly in the refrigerator first, then pack it in a cooler surrounded by ice packs. Be especially cautious with perishable food, specifically meat, seafood, and eggs. Pack any raw meat in drip-proof containers at the bottom of the cooler, in case of spills; this will help to avoid contaminating everything else. The ideal temperature to store perishable food is 40°F or below.

- Never partly cook something to finish off at the picnic. Bacteria thrive in moderate temperatures.

- Pack a cooler with food in the order that it will be used to keep the food cool until it's needed. Try to pack coolers full. A full cooler will stay colder longer.
- When transporting food in a car, keep the perishable items inside where it's air-conditioned rather than in the hot trunk.

At the Picnic

- Set up the food in a shaded area. If there's no shaded area, pitch a tent or a canopy. Keep hot foods hot and cold foods cold. Have a separate cooler for drinks and one for foods. Coolers that contain drinks tend to be opened and closed all day, decreasing the internal temperature.
- Never leave food out for over two hours. If the weather is over 90°F outside, don't leave anything out longer than one hour. Avoid the temptation to bring perishable leftovers home.
- When taking food off of the grill, place it in a clean container, not the container used to store the meat before it was cooked. Never serve the meat's marinade without bringing it to a good boil first.

Washing Up

- Wash hands before and after preparing food. If there are no facilities in the area, bring moist towelettes or antibacterial gel.
- When cooking with raw meat, especially in an area without hot water for washing up, bring a mixture of 1/4 cup bleach to one gallon of water in a spray bottle. Use it to wipe down cutting boards until you can wash them properly back at home.

PACKING LIST

- picnic blankets, woven mats
- tablecloths or oil cloth
- utensils if necessary (plastic or not)
- serrated knife
- corkscrew and bottle opener
- cutting board
- napkins
- paper towels
- antibacterial gel
- towelettes
- lock-top storage bags
- trash bags for cleaning up
- ice or ice packs
- cooler
- insect repellent
- citronella candles
- sunscreen
- tent or umbrella
- salt and pepper shakers
- condiments
- plenty of water and beverages

GRILLING

- small grill or hibachi
- lighter or matches
- fire starter or lighter fluid
- tongs and spatula
- spray bottle of water (for flare-ups on the grill)
- extra platter for cooked meats
- oils or seasonings
- charcoal or wood chips

BITS AND BITES

SOME OF THE BEST PICNICS ARE MADE UP OF BITS AND BITES of this and that: A nibble here of good and salty prosciutto draped over a juicy slice of melon, a bite there of bracing crisp pickles, and a handful of pine nuts and pecans. Select a couple of these recipes as the prelude to a meal or make them the main attraction.

Spiced Pine Nuts, Pecans, and Pumpkin Seeds

A variation on the usual nut mix of almonds, walnuts, and pecans, this makes a great trail mix as much as a good nibble to serve with cheese and a glass of wine.

2 tablespoons butter

1 teaspoon kosher salt

½ teaspoon ground cumin

½ teaspoon cayenne pepper

1 cup pecan halves (about 4 ounces)

¾ cup pine nuts (about 4 ounces)

¾ cup pumpkin seeds (about 3 ounces)

Preheat the oven to 350°F. Melt the butter in a small sauté pan and stir in the salt, cumin, and cayenne. Remove from the heat.

Combine the pecans, pine nuts, and pumpkin seeds in a medium bowl and toss the butter and spice mixture with the nuts. Spread the nuts on a baking sheet in a single layer, and roast for 10 minutes. Remove to a plate to let cool. Keep stored in a well-sealed plastic container.

SERVES 6

Quick Pickled Veggies

Crunchy and colorful, these pickles can be made from any mix of crisp vegetables. The garlic and ginger give them a good bit of heat. Refrigerated, they'll keep nicely for up to a week. Serve with cheese and cured meats for a light lunch.

2 cups small cauliflower florets

2 cups ½-inch-thick carrot slices

2 cups 1-inch-thick small zucchini slices

1 cup 1-inch green bell pepper squares

1 cup 1-inch red bell pepper squares

2 sprigs fresh tarragon

2½ cups water

1½ cups white wine vinegar

¾ cup unseasoned rice vinegar

⅔ cup sugar

2½-inch piece fresh ginger, peeled and cut into thin slices

7 cloves garlic, peeled and halved

1 tablespoon kosher salt

2 teaspoons yellow mustard seeds

1½ teaspoons red pepper flakes

Combine the vegetables and the tarragon in a large, nonreactive bowl or wide-mouthed jar and set aside. Bring the water, wine vinegar, rice vinegar, sugar, ginger, garlic, salt, mustard seeds, and red pepper flakes to a boil in a large pot. Reduce to a simmer and cook for 10 minutes. Bring to a boil again and pour the hot liquid over the vegetables. Stir occasionally while the mixture cools, then cover and refrigerate. Wait at least 3 days before eating, stirring every once in a while to keep all of the vegetables submerged. When serving, make sure to avoid the ginger and warn people about the garlic.

SERVES 6 TO 8

Mixed Olives with Orange and Coriander

Long slivers of orange and lemon peel and a mixture of green and black olives of all sizes make this mix as pretty to look at as it is addictive to eat. For green olives, look for picholine; for black olives, tiny, mild niçoise and big meaty kalamata are easy to find. Make sure to purchase unseasoned olives, packed in brine rather than dried.

2 cups unpitted olives, a mixture of both green and black, large and small

2 tablespoons olive oil

6 thin strips of lemon peel

6 thin strips of orange peel

2 cloves garlic, cut into thin slices

1 teaspoon freshly squeezed lemon juice

¼ teaspoon finely chopped orange zest

¼ teaspoon finely chopped lemon zest

¼ teaspoon whole coriander seeds

1 bay leaf

Combine all the ingredients in a medium bowl, cover, and marinate refrigerated for at least 2 days, stirring occasionally.

SERVES 6

Curried Deviled Eggs

This timeless picnic favorite is given a bit of zip with the addition of curry powder and lemon juice. For an elegant picnic, try using tiny quail eggs and piping the filling in; they're a bit more labor intensive, but irresistible. When transporting deviled eggs, make sure that they are covered well with plastic wrap and kept in a cooler.

12 large eggs at room temperature

⅔ cup mayonnaise

2 tablespoons freshly squeezed lemon juice

1½ teaspoons curry powder

Kosher salt

Freshly ground black pepper

Chopped chives for garnish

To hard-boil the eggs, place in a large pot of cold water and bring to a boil. Remove from the heat, cover, and let sit for 15 to 20 minutes. Drain carefully and let cool before shelling them.

Slice the eggs in half lengthwise and remove the yolks, placing them in a large bowl. Place the egg white halves on a serving plate. To the yolks, add the mayonnaise, lemon juice, and curry powder. Use a fork to mash well and combine. Season to taste with salt and pepper.

Using a spoon, fill the egg whites with generous spoonfuls of the egg yolk mixture, dividing evenly. Sprinkle with chopped chives for garnish. Cover and keep refrigerated until ready to serve.

SERVES 12

Prosciutto and Melon

It seems like every trattoria in Italy offers prosciutto, the salt-cured Italian ham, draped over fresh melon. It's a lovely combination of sweet and salty. Although there's no cooking involved, it does require using the ripest fruit and highest quality prosciutto (prosciutto de Parma is considered the best) sliced as thin as a piece of silk. As an alternative to prosciutto, you could try thinly sliced Smithfield ham. Try using other mild fruits such as fresh figs or white peaches. Pack the sliced melon in an airtight container and assemble with the prosciutto at the picnic.

1 ripe cantaloupe or other melon, seeded and cut into eight 2-inch-thick wedges

8 thin slices prosciutto

When ready to serve, drape the prosciutto over the wedges of melon.

SERVES 4

Crusty Focaccia with Rosemary

This thin and crusty focaccia, based on a recipe by respected pastry chef and cookbook author Nick Malgieri, is a world away from the fluffy, doughy versions of focaccia that have become ubiquitous. It's perfect for sandwiches—use two pieces because it's too thin to slice in half. The dough will seem sticky and sparse, but just grease your hands with olive oil and trust that it will work. Once you master this basic recipe, try dotting the dough with olive halves or sliced onions.

5 tablespoons extra-virgin olive oil, plus extra for greasing

4 cups all-purpose flour

3½ teaspoons kosher salt, plus more to taste

2 cups warm water

1 envelope dry yeast (not fast-acting or rapid rise)

¼ teaspoon sugar

2 teaspoons roughly chopped fresh rosemary

Generously grease the bottom and sides of a baking pan with shallow sides, approximately 13 by 17 by 1 inch.

Combine the flour and 2 teaspoons of the salt in a large bowl and mix well. In a small bowl, mix together the warm water, yeast, and sugar, and allow to proof for 10 minutes, or until it becomes foamy. Whisk in 2 tablespoons of the olive oil. Add the yeast mixture to the flour mixture and mix with a wooden spoon until the dough is totally smooth and silky, about 1 minute.

Cover the bowl with oiled plastic wrap and allow the dough to rise until double, approximately 1 hour.

Carefully scrape the dough into the pan. Rub your hands with olive oil to keep them from sticking and press and spread the dough until it covers the whole pan. (It will seem thin.) Cover with oiled plastic wrap and allow to rise until double, approximately 1 hour. Preheat the oven to 450°F.

Just before baking, using your fingertips, make indentations—or dimples—about 1 inch apart, all over the focaccia. Drizzle 2 tablespoons of the olive oil over the top. Sprinkle the remaining 1½ teaspoons of salt and the rosemary over the top.

Bake 20 minutes, or until golden brown. Remove from the oven and brush the top lightly with the remaining 1 tablespoon of olive oil. Remove from the pan, using a spatula to loosen any spots that stick. Salt to taste. Cool on a wire rack.

SERVES 6 TO 8

Cheese Course

Sometimes the most pleasurable picnics are the no-cook ones: just a smattering of cheese, fruit, and cured meats, plus a baguette and, of course, a nice bottle of wine. Although there are no hard rules for cheese pairings, below are some no-fail plans. When selecting your cheeses, look for a nice mix, such as a mild cheese, a strong cheese, a soft washed-rind cheese, and hard cheese—and it's always fun to mix up your milk base, whether it be goat's milk, sheep's milk, or cow's milk. Don't forget that not all cheeses can stand high heat or being squashed in a backpack full of other goods. If you're hiking in hot weather to your picnic spot, avoid something like soft Brie—otherwise, you'll have a puddle of cheese when you get there. When selecting breads and crackers, steer clear of highly salted versions; you don't want the flavor of the crackers to compete with the flavor of the cheese.

Try these winning flavor pairings:

- **Parmesan, or a similar hard, nutty-flavored crumbly cheese with sticky sweet dates or quince paste**
- **Pungent blues, such as Gorgonzola, with sliced apples or red grapes**
- **Mild, soft-ripened cheese, such as Teleme, with cherries**
- **Fresh cheeses such as ricotta or fromage blanc with berries**
- **Fresh, tangy goat's milk cheeses with fresh figs, honey, and walnut bread**
- **Gorgonzola with honey or pears and raisin bread**
- **Roquefort with toasted walnuts and ripe pears**
- **English-style Cheddar with chutneys and pickled onions**
- **Shaved pecorino with fresh shelled fava beans (try shelled soy beans as an alternative)**
- **Fennel wedges with Reblochon or another mild, cow's milk cheese**

When purchasing the cheese, figure that each person will eat about 3 ounces. Pack any soft cheeses in a protective hard container with a lid; a cardboard box will work, as will a plastic container. Don't place ice packs or ice directly on the cheeses; you don't want them to get wet. Keep cheeses cool while transporting, but once you're ready to serve, let them sit out until they come to room temperature before eating. It's a good idea to bring along a small cutting board and cheese knife, too.

Avocado-Tomatillo Salsa

A classic combination in Mexico, this is a great (and less time consuming) alternative to the more common salsa fresca made with chopped fresh tomatoes. Tomatillos, which look like mini green tomatoes covered with a papery husk, are part of the nightshade family. They're readily available in almost any Latin market, but are quickly becoming common in mainstream supermarkets, too. Look for ones with smooth, undimpled skin. Serve the salsa with tortillas chips or as a sauce for grilled meats or fish.

10 tomatillos (6 ounces), husked

½ cup chopped onion, preferably sweet, such as Vidalia

1 small clove garlic, chopped

½ fresh jalapeño, chopped (optional)

2 ripe avocados (about 1 pound), peeled and pitted

Kosher salt

1 tablespoon freshly squeezed lemon juice

Place the tomatillos in a small pot of simmering water. Cook until the tomatillos are soft, about 10 minutes depending on size. Drain and place in a blender or food processor. Add the onion, garlic, and jalapeño, if using, and blend or process until smooth.

In a medium bowl, use a fork to roughly mash the meat of the avocados. Add the tomatillo purée and combine. Season to taste with salt and add lemon juice as desired. If necessary, thin with a little water; the consistency shouldn't be too thick. Refrigerate in a container with plastic wrap laid directly onto the salsa to keep it from discoloring.

SERVES 6 TO 8; MAKES ABOUT 2 CUPS

SIMPLY SANDWICHES

SANDWICHES WERE MADE FOR PICNICS: PORTABLE AND satisfying, they're a meal between two slices of bread. But not all sandwiches are created equal. The most delicious ones aren't piled high with novel combinations, they're made simply using the best ingredients: summer-ripe tomatoes, freshly roasted meat, a quality baguette. Keep it basic and you'll be glad you did.

Fresh Mozzarella, Tomato, and Basil Sandwich

I like this simple, summery sandwich best served on herbed focaccia drizzled with good, peppery extra-virgin olive oil. (If using the Crusty Focaccia with Rosemary from page 21, no extra olive oil is necessary.) Fresh mozzarella, packed in water or whey, is available in most grocery stores but tends to be undersalted; make sure to season your sandwich well. For something a little more special, make the sandwich with a couple different varieties of basil, such as purple basil or lemon basil, or even a swipe of fresh (homemade or store-bought) pesto. If making a few hours ahead, choose a sturdier bread, like a baguette; it won't get soggy as quickly.

4 pieces of bread such as focaccia or baguette, halved

4 teaspoons extra-virgin olive oil

1 large clove garlic, halved

1 pound large fresh mozzarella balls, cut into thick slices

Kosher salt

Freshly ground black pepper

2 large tomatoes, cut into slices

1 bunch fresh basil, leaves separated

Brush the bottom half of each piece of bread with olive oil and rub with the cut end of the garlic. Top with a layer of mozzarella and sprinkle with salt and pepper. Top with the tomato slices and sprinkle with salt and pepper again. Top with basil leaves. Brush the remaining bread with olive oil and place on top.

SERVES 4

Pan Bagnat with Tuna, Tomatoes, and Olives

This stuffed sandwich is traditionally found on the beaches of Nice, France. The beauty of a pan bagnat is that it's pressed, soaking the crusty French bread with olive oil and the juice of ripe summer tomatoes, until it becomes soft and the flavors are melded. Use good-quality canned tuna packed in olive oil.

DRESSING

2½ tablespoons red wine vinegar

1 tablespoon brined capers, drained and roughly chopped

1½ teaspoons anchovy paste

½ teaspoon sugar

½ cup extra-virgin olive oil

4 crusty French rolls, halved

2 large cloves garlic, halved

2 large tomatoes, cut into thick slices

Kosher salt

4 large eggs, hard-boiled and cut into thin slices

8 radishes, cut into thin slices

One 6- to 7-ounce can olive oil–packed tuna

16 pitted kalamata olives, flattened

1 red onion, cut into thin slices and divided into rings

16 large basil leaves

To make the dressing: Combine the vinegar, capers, anchovy paste, and sugar in a medium bowl. Whisk in the olive oil.

Brush both of the cut sides of the bread with the dressing, reserving a little for later. Rub the cut sides of the bread with the garlic.

On the bottom half of each piece of bread, place a layer of tomatoes, salting them lightly. Follow with slices of boiled egg, sliced radishes, a quarter of the tuna (followed by a drizzle of the remaining dressing), 4 olives, rings of red onion, and 4 basil leaves.

Top with the remaining pieces of bread and wrap each sandwich tightly with plastic wrap. To press it, place something heavy on top and place in the refrigerator for 2 hours. The resulting sandwich should be moist, but not so much that the bottom crust is soaked through.

SERVES 4

Vietnamese Chicken Sandwich with Carrot-Daikon Slaw

This sandwich is a delicious collision of French and Vietnamese cultures. Known in Vietnam as *banh mi,* it usually includes some kind of meat, such as cinnamon-scented pâté or grilled pork, piled on a baguette. But what really makes a *banh mi* addictive is the crunchy slaw made of pickled carrots and daikon radish. The best way to slice the vegetables is with a Japanese mandoline—if you don't have one, they're an inexpensive investment and make slicing and julienning a cinch. Daikon, a long, large, white Asian radish, is commonly found in both Asian and Western markets. If you're in a rush, use leftover chicken and skip the marinade.

SLAW

8 ounces carrots, peeled

8 ounces daikon, peeled

1½ cups water

2 tablespoons sugar

1 teaspoon kosher salt

1½ pounds skinless, boneless chicken thighs or breasts

MARINADE

⅓ cup warm water

¼ cup fish sauce

3 tablespoons freshly squeezed lime juice

2 tablespoons sugar

1 teaspoon chopped garlic

3 thin round slices fresh jalapeño

6 crusty French rolls or wide pieces of baguette, halved

Mayonnaise

Asian chili sauce (optional)

Fish sauce

1 bunch cilantro, tough stems trimmed

Sliced jalapeños (optional)

To make the slaw: Using a mandoline, cut the carrots and daikon into julienne (or matchsticks); alternatively, shred long on the big holes of a box grater. In a medium bowl, combine the water, sugar, and salt. Mix until dissolved. Add the carrots and daikon. Cover and chill in the refrigerator for at least an hour. Drain well before assembling the sandwiches.

Bring a large pot of lightly salted water to a boil and reduce to a gentle simmer. If using chicken thighs, trim off any extra fat. Add the chicken to the simmering water. Poach for 15 minutes, or until cooked through. Remove the chicken from the water, let cool, and use your fingers or a knife to shred. Set aside.

To make the marinade: In a large bowl, combine the water, fish sauce, lime juice, sugar, garlic, and jalapeño. Stir to dissolve the sugar. Add the chicken, mix, and let sit at room temperature for 20 minutes, or cover and chill for an hour.

Take the bottom half of each piece of bread and spread with mayonnaise and if desired, some chili sauce. Sprinkle lightly with fish sauce. Top with some cilantro (including some of the tender stems is fine), a generous amount of chicken, and some of the well-drained carrot and daikon slaw. If desired, add slices of jalapeño. Spread a little mayonnaise on the remaining pieces of bread and place on top.

SERVES 6

Roasted Pork Sandwich with Fennel and Apple

Stuffed with rosemary, sage, and fennel, this is the best roast pork you'll ever have. While many pork roasts are made with the loin, a lean cut that tends to get dry, this recipe uses pork butt, also called pork shoulder, which stays moist and tender. (If it's not available, ask your butcher to prepare a shoulder roast for you, rolled and tied.) The pork also makes a sophisticated dinner for two the night before and at least four fantastic leftover sandwiches the next day. Take note that it needs to be prepared the day before roasting it, in order to allow the flavors to infuse. The sandwich is best suited for flavorful, more rustic breads.

1 tablespoon coarsely chopped garlic

1 tablespoon finely chopped fresh rosemary

1 tablespoon finely chopped fresh sage

1 tablespoon coarsely ground black pepper

1 tablespoon fennel seeds

1½ teaspoons kosher salt

3 pounds rolled and tied pork butt (shoulder)

¼ cup olive oil

½ cup chicken stock (optional)

12 slices of bread, such as pain au levain or light rye

Dijon whole-grain mustard

Mayonnaise

1 fennel bulb, trimmed and cut into thin slices

1 tart apple, such as Granny Smith, cored and cut into thin slices

Combine the garlic, rosemary, sage, pepper, fennel seeds, and salt in a small bowl. Use your hands to gently stuff the spice mixture into every nook and cranny that you can find between the muscles of the meat. If you feel there are parts of the pork that haven't been seasoned enough, simply use a paring knife to put a small 1-inch-deep slit into the meat, following the natural seams, and add more of the spice mixture. Wrap with plastic wrap and refrigerate the pork for 24 hours or up to 3 days (the longer the better).

Before roasting, give yourself at least 30 minutes to bring the pork to room temperature. Preheat the oven to 350°F. Add the olive oil in a large roasting pan in the oven. When the oil is hot, about 10 minutes, add the pork roast. Roast uncovered for 1 hour and, using tongs, turn to an unbrowned side. Roast another hour and turn again. Continue roasting until the meat has reached an internal temperature of about 185°F, 15 to 30 minutes longer, for a total roasting time of about 2½ hours. Remove the pork and set aside to cool, saving the juices in the pan.

(For an extra delicious sandwich, place the roasting pan over medium heat, add the chicken stock to the juices in the roasting pan and use a spatula to scrape off any bits of pork and drippings stuck to the bottom. Bring to a quick boil and pour into a shallow bowl.)

To prepare the sandwiches, allow the roast to cool, then thinly slice the pork. If using the sauce, dip the pork slices into the sauce to get them extra juicy. Take the bottom halves of the bread and spread with your choice of mustard or mayonnaise. Top with lots of pork, sliced fennel, and apple. Spread the remaining bread slices with mustard or mayonnaise and place on top.

SERVES 6

Grilled Skirt Steak Sandwich with Salsa Verde

Salsa verde, piquant with capers and salty with anchovies, is a classic match with grilled steak. The steak can be grilled ahead of time—even the day before; just wait to slice it until you're ready to make the sandwiches. An even tastier option is to bring the marinated meat and grill it at the picnic, letting people assemble their own sandwiches there.

SALSA VERDE

2½ cups finely chopped fresh Italian parsley

¼ cup finely chopped shallots

3 tablespoons red wine vinegar

3 tablespoons brined capers, drained and chopped

2½ teaspoons anchovy paste

¾ cup extra-virgin olive oil

2 teaspoons kosher salt

¾ teaspoon freshly ground black pepper

2 tablespoons extra-virgin olive oil

1 tablespoon finely chopped garlic

2 teaspoons kosher salt

½ teaspoon freshly ground black pepper

2½ pounds skirt steak

6 French rolls or pieces of focaccia, halved

1 red onion, cut into thin slices, for dressing

Trimmed watercress for dressing

To make the Salsa Verde: Combine the parsley, shallots, vinegar, capers, and anchovy paste in a medium bowl. Slowly whisk in the olive oil. Add the salt and pepper. Covered and refrigerated, the salsa can be kept for several days.

In a small bowl, combine the olive oil, garlic, salt, and pepper and rub the steak with it. Cover with plastic wrap and let marinate in the refrigerator for 1 hour. Prepare a grill for a hot fire. Place the steak over direct heat and grill 3 to 4 minutes per side for medium-rare. Remove to a cutting board. When cool, slice the steak across the grain into thin strips, at the most ½ inch thick.

Take each bottom half of the bread and spread it with generous amounts of the Salsa Verde. Top with slices of steak, onion, watercress leaves, and the remaining pieces of bread.

SERVES 6

Meatloaf Sandwich with Chipotle Mayonnaise

Meatloaf is one of those things that's worth making the night before, just so you can make sandwiches with it the next day. Here, Italian sausage gives it a good kick, as does the addition of smoky, spicy chipotle mayonnaise. To make fresh bread crumbs, cut off the crusts from good-quality white bread. Tear into chunks, place in a food processor, and pulse a few times. If you can't find Italian sausage sold unstuffed, just slice open a couple links of sausage and remove the meat. Chipotle chiles are smoked jalapeños; for this recipe, look for them sold in small cans packed in sweet-spicy adobo sauce.

MEATLOAF

2 tablespoons extra-virgin olive oil

1½ cups chopped onion

1 tablespoon chopped garlic

1½ pounds ground beef

1 pound ground dark meat turkey

8 ounces spicy Italian sausage

2 cups fresh white bread crumbs

½ cup whole milk

2 large eggs, lightly beaten

1 tablespoon chopped fresh oregano

1 tablespoon chopped fresh sage

2 teaspoons kosher salt

½ teaspoon freshly ground black pepper

CHIPOTLE MAYONNAISE

1 cup mayonnaise

2 teaspoons adobo sauce from canned chipotles, or to taste

12 slices good-quality hearty white or wheat sandwich bread

To make the meatloaf: Preheat the oven to 350°F. Heat the olive oil in a skillet over medium heat. Add the onion and garlic and cook for 10 minutes, or until beginning to brown. Remove and let cool.

In a large bowl, combine the beef, turkey, sausage, bread crumbs, milk, eggs, oregano, sage, salt, and pepper. Add the garlic and onion mixture. Use your hands to mix it all together until just combined.

Shape the meat into about a 10-by-5-by-2-inch loaf in a large shallow baking pan. Bake for 50 to 60 minutes, or until no longer pink in the middle. Remove from the oven and cool. Cover with plastic wrap and refrigerate overnight or until chilled. Slice to make sandwiches.

To make the Chipotle Mayonnaise: In a small bowl, combine the mayonnaise and adobo sauce.

Take the bottom halves of the bread, and spread them with a good amount of the Chipotle Mayonnaise. Add a thick slice or 2 of the meatloaf and top with the remaining bread. Either enjoy as is, or add other fixings, such as ketchup, tomatoes, lettuce, and onion. Although this sandwich can be made ahead, it's also fun to let people make their own at the picnic, especially if you use all the fixings.

SERVES 6 WITH LEFTOVERS

Roasted Eggplant and Bell Pepper Sandwich with Herbed Goat Cheese

This vegetarian sandwich pleases both meat and veggie lovers alike. For different variations, try roasting thin, long slices of zucchini or slices of red onion. You can substitute globe eggplant, sliced into rounds, for the Japanese eggplant. These sandwiches can be assembled ahead of time.

¼ cup extra-virgin olive oil, plus extra for greasing

4 large Japanese eggplants (about 12 ounces)

Kosher salt

2 large red bell peppers

5 ounces fresh goat cheese at room temperature

3 tablespoons plain whole-milk yogurt

2 tablespoons chopped fresh chives

2 tablespoons chopped fresh oregano

Freshly ground black pepper

4 pieces of bread, such as focaccia or baguette, halved

Baby arugula for dressing (optional)

Preheat the oven to 400°F. Brush a baking sheet with olive oil.

Trim the stem end off of the eggplants and slice each eggplant lengthwise into ½-inch-thick slices. Brush both sides of the eggplant slices with olive oil and place on the baking sheet. Salt liberally.

Slice the bell peppers in half through the stem end. Trim and devein, removing the seeds. Place the bell peppers cut-side down on the baking sheet.

Roast until the eggplant is tender, 15 to 20 minutes. Use a spatula to remove the eggplant to a plate. Return the peppers to the oven and cook until tender, 15 minutes more. Place the bell peppers on another plate. Cover with a plastic bag and let steam until cool. Remove the skin and slice on the diagonal into thick slices.

In a small bowl, combine the goat cheese, yogurt, chives, and oregano. Mix well and season to taste with salt and pepper.

Spread the bottom half of each piece of bread with a good amount of the herbed goat cheese. Top with a layer of eggplant and bell pepper, plus the arugula, if using, and season lightly with salt and pepper. Spread the remaining bread with the rest of the goat cheese and place on top.

SERVES 4

SALADS AND SIDES

AS MUCH AS A PICNIC MIGHT NOT SEEM LIKE A PICNIC without a taste of some all-American potato salad or coleslaw, think outside the box sometimes—there's a whole world of salads and sides to choose from. Try crisp green beans with an almond-ginger dressing, a French-inspired dish of lentils and beets, or even a cold gazpacho from Spain. The only thing to avoid is a salad made with delicate leafy greens, which on a hot day might take a beating from the sun.

Green Beans with Almond Butter–Ginger Dressing

Green beans are often paired with toasted almonds, but tossed with this creamy almond butter dressing, it's double the pleasure. Almond butter can be found in health food stores and gourmet markets; ideally, look for the kind that has already been emulsified and doesn't have to be mixed by hand. Mirin, a Japanese sweet rice wine, is available in most gourmet markets. Don't skip the toasted almonds strewn over the salad; they look beautiful and add a necessary crunch.

DRESSING

2-inch piece fresh ginger, peeled

½ cup creamy, unsweetened almond butter

5 tablespoons mirin

¼ cup unseasoned rice wine vinegar

2 tablespoons soy sauce

1 teaspoon kosher salt

2 pounds trimmed green beans

1 cup sliced natural almonds (about 4 ounces)

To make the dressing: Using a small-holed grater, such as a Parmesan grater, grate the fresh ginger over a medium bowl in order to catch the juice and the pulp. You should have about 1 teaspoon. To the same bowl, add the almond butter, mirin, vinegar, soy sauce, and salt. Use a whisk or fork to combine well.

Add the green beans to a large pot of lightly salted boiling water. Cook for 3 to 5 minutes, or until crisp-tender. Drain in a colander and rinse under cold water to stop the cooking.

In a large dry skillet over medium heat, add the almonds. Stir constantly, about 5 minutes, until fragrant and lightly toasted. Remove from heat and let cool on a plate. In a large bowl, toss the green beans with the dressing, using as much dressing as desired, and scatter it with the almonds. Alternatively, bring the almonds and dressing to the picnic in separate containers and wait to toss them with the green beans until ready to serve.

SERVES 6 TO 8

French Lentils with Roasted Beets and Pancetta

French lentils (versus the more common brown, red, or yellow) are necessary for this recipe. They still have their seed coat, and unlike other lentils, they don't easily turn to mush. Although you certainly could use red beets, I prefer golden beets because they don't dye everything they touch a shade of pink. To keep the fried pancetta crisp, pack it for the picnic in a separate container, tossing it with the salad at the last minute. Bacon would work as an alternative. Although the crumbled fresh goat cheese is optional, it makes this salad all the more delicious.

1 pound golden beets, trimmed

1½ cups dried French lentils

¼ of a small onion

1 clove garlic, crushed

1 bay leaf

1 teaspoon kosher salt

1 tablespoon extra-virgin olive oil

8 slices pancetta

⅓ cup chopped fresh parsley

⅓ cup crumbled fresh goat cheese (optional)

DRESSING

½ cup extra-virgin olive oil

¼ cup red wine vinegar

1 clove garlic, crushed

Kosher salt

Freshly ground black pepper

Preheat the oven to 400°F. Place the beets in a roasting pan and fill with about ½ inch of water. Cover with foil and roast for 1 hour, or until a knife inserted into the center of a beet indicates that it's cooked through. Remove from the oven. Let cool and slip the skins off. Cut into ½-inch cubes.

Rinse the lentils, removing any pebbles. Place in a pot with water to cover and bring to a boil. Reduce to a simmer, and add the onion, garlic, bay leaf, and salt. Simmer, uncovered, for 20 to 30 minutes, or until the lentils are just tender (they'll still be slightly firm). Remove from the heat and let sit for 10 minutes. Drain off any remaining water in a colander and remove the onion, garlic, and bay leaf. Let cool.

(continued)

Heat the olive oil in a sauté pan over medium heat and add the pancetta. Sauté for 5 to 10 minutes, or until crisp. Remove to a paper towel, let cool, and use your hands to crumble.

To make the dressing: Whisk together the olive oil and vinegar with the garlic. Season to taste with salt and pepper and let sit for about 10 minutes to infuse the garlic, whisking again before dressing the lentils. Remove the garlic.

To assemble the salad: Toss together the lentils, beets, and parsley, adding the dressing as desired. Taste and adjust the seasoning with salt and pepper if necessary. Toss with the pancetta and goat cheese, if using, just before serving.

SERVES 4 TO 6

Orzo Salad with Green Olives, Tomatoes, and Feta

Orzo, rice-sized grains of pasta, makes an ideal salad. This version is Greek-inspired, full of green olives, cucumber, tomatoes, and feta, but just about anything could be included, from chopped radishes to blanched chopped green beans, peas, or broccoli florets.

1 pound uncooked orzo (2 generous cups)

¼ cup olive oil

2 pounds cherry tomatoes in an assortment of colors, halved

2 teaspoons kosher salt

1 English cucumber, unpeeled, quartered lengthwise and cut into slices

1 cup chopped red onion

1 cup (about 5 ounces) feta cheese, crumbled

¾ cup green olives, halved

½ cup chopped fresh Italian parsley

¼ cup freshly squeezed lemon juice

½ teaspoon freshly ground black pepper

Bring a large pot of salted water to a boil. Add the orzo and cook until just tender, about 8 minutes. Drain. Rinse with cold water and drain again. Add 2 tablespoons of the olive oil and mix well. Set aside.

Put the tomatoes in a large bowl and add 1 teaspoon of the salt. Let stand for ½ hour or so and then drain any accumulated liquid. Add the cucumber, red onion, feta, olives, parsley, lemon juice, and the remaining 2 tablespoons olive oil and gently mix. Add the orzo and gently toss with the vegetables. Season with the remaining salt and the pepper. Cover and refrigerate until ready to serve.

SERVES 6

Chopped Spring Salad with Asparagus and Peas

What better way to celebrate the spring than with this salad made with the best pick of the season, in every shade of green? Although the avocado can be left out entirely, if using, make sure to bring it to the picnic whole, cutting and tossing it with the salad at the last minute to keep it from turning brown and mushy. If it's going to be over an hour before you serve the salad, it's best to pack the dressing separately as well and dress the salad on location; this will keep it bright and green.

2½ tablespoons freshly squeezed lemon juice

2 tablespoons olive oil

1 clove garlic, crushed

Kosher salt

Freshly ground black pepper

1 pound asparagus

1 cup fresh or frozen peas

½ English cucumber, unpeeled, quartered lengthwise and sliced

3 green onions, white part only, cut into thin slices

1 ripe, slightly firm avocado, peeled, pitted, and cut into 1-inch dice (optional)

In a small jar with a lid, combine the lemon juice, olive oil, and garlic. Shake well and season with salt and pepper. Set aside.

Snap the tough bottoms off of the asparagus where they break naturally, then trim and slice the asparagus on a diagonal into 1-inch pieces. Blanch in a medium pot of lightly salted boiling water for 1½ minutes. Use a strainer to remove and run the asparagus under cold water to stop the cooking. Set aside.

Using the same boiling water, blanch the peas for about 30 seconds if fresh and 10 seconds if frozen. Drain, run under cold water, and set aside. In a portable container or serving bowl, combine the asparagus, peas, cucumber, onions, and if serving immediately, the avocado (if using). Reshake the dressing and toss gently with the salad. Season with salt and pepper and serve.

SERVES 6 TO 8

Quick Summertime Gazpacho

This soup is only as good as its ingredients, especially the tomatoes. Make sure that they're in season and even better, homegrown. Use the lazy cook's approach and simply peel them with a sharp peeler rather than blanching them to remove the skin. Try serving with a couple garnishes, such as diced cucumbers, sliced red and yellow cherry tomatoes, chopped green olives, chopped hard-boiled eggs, or capers. To keep it chilled, bring this to a picnic in a thermos. To double this recipe, blend the gazpacho in two batches.

4 large tomatoes (about 1½ pounds)

1½ cups peeled and chopped English cucumber

1 cup chopped red onion

½ cup extra-virgin olive oil

2 tablespoons white wine vinegar

1 teaspoon chopped garlic

Kosher salt

Freshly ground black pepper

Tabasco

Core the tomatoes. Using a sharp peeler, peel off the skin. Roughly chop.

Place the tomatoes, cucumber, onion, olive oil, vinegar, and garlic in the blender. Blend until puréed. Season with salt, pepper, and Tabasco. Chill in the refrigerator, 1 hour or as long as overnight. This gazpacho is even better when served the next day.

SERVES 4

Old-Fashioned Coleslaw with Apples

Although apples might seem like a new twist on this traditional recipe, a lot of old cookbooks include coleslaw recipes with apple in them. A mix of carrots, plus green and red cabbage, makes this recipe as colorful as it is tasty. If making a day ahead (it will still be good but a little more wilted), substitute green for the red cabbage because the red cabbage will eventually turn the whole salad pink.

1 large tart green apple, such as Granny Smith, cored, peeled, and diced

1 tablespoon freshly squeezed lemon juice

4 cups shredded green cabbage

1 cup shredded red cabbage

1 cup shredded carrots

½ cup chopped radishes

DRESSING

½ cup mayonnaise

2 tablespoons sugar

2 tablespoons white wine vinegar

2 teaspoons celery seed

1 teaspoon kosher salt

¼ teaspoon freshly ground black pepper

Combine the apple with the lemon juice in a large nonreactive bowl and mix thoroughly. Add the green and red cabbage, carrots, and radishes.

To make the dressing: In a small bowl, stir together the mayonnaise and sugar until the sugar is dissolved. Add the vinegar, celery seed, salt, and pepper. Add the dressing to the vegetables and gently toss to coat. Cover and chill until ready to serve.

SERVES 6

Melon Skewers with Lime and Mint

From Crenshaw to orange honeydew, French Charentais to yellow watermelon, it seems like our choice of different varieties of melons expands every summer. This handheld fruit salad is best made using an assortment of melons, but any mix of fruit, such as pineapple, nectarines, or papaya, will work well too. To transport the melon, either assemble the skewers at your picnic spot or pack them in long, boxy airtight plastic containers.

1 cup water

½ cup sugar

½ cup freshly squeezed orange juice

½ cup freshly squeezed lime juice

5 sprigs fresh mint

10 cups of 1-inch melon cubes, seeded, preferably a mix of varieties and colors

In a small saucepan, bring the water and sugar to a boil and simmer uncovered for 2 to 3 minutes. Remove from the heat and let cool.

In a large bowl, add the orange juice, lime juice, and mint to the melon. Pour the cooled syrup over the melon, stir gently, cover, and refrigerate for several hours to allow the flavors to marry. Thread the melon onto 24 ten-inch skewers, alternating colors, and serve.

SERVES 12

Mangoes with Chile, Lemon, and Salt

In Mexico, the unlikely combination of sweet fruit, such as watermelon or mango, paired with chile powder, lemon juice, and salt makes a bracing, but refreshing summer treat. It's one of those things you have to try to believe, and then you're hooked. If you can find Manila mangoes, a small, more almond-shaped variety, snap them up; they have the most creamy flesh and tart-sweet flavor. Either serve within a couple hours or prepare the mangoes at the picnic. They're meant to be eaten with your hands.

6 ripe mangoes

2 tablespoons kosher salt

2 tablespoons chile powder

2 lemons, cut into wedges

Take a mango, and slice off the 2 fleshiest sides, running your knife down, as close as you can, to the long narrow seed (leave the skin on). Take each mango half, flesh-side up, and use a paring knife to score the mango into cubes. Twist the mango inside out so that the cubes of flesh stick out. Repeat with the rest of the mangoes.

When ready to serve, place the scored mango halves on a serving platter, accompanied by small bowls of the salt and the chile powder. Place the lemon wedges around the mangoes. To serve, encourage people to sprinkle a little salt, a little chile, and a squeeze of lemon on their mango halves and eat with their hands.

SERVES 6

German-Style Potato Salad with Bacon and Mustard

Dressed with vinegar and whole-grain mustard instead of mayonnaise, this pretty potato salad is a great side dish for grilled sausages. To make a vegetarian version, just omit the bacon and sauté the onions and thyme in a few tablespoons of olive oil.

3½ pounds small red potatoes

8 pieces bacon

2 cups chopped yellow onions

1 tablespoon chopped fresh thyme

⅓ cup chopped fresh parsley

DRESSING

½ cup cider vinegar

¼ cup extra-virgin olive oil

2 tablespoons whole-grain Dijon mustard

½ teaspoon sugar

Kosher salt

Freshly ground black pepper

Place the potatoes in a large pot of lightly salted, cold water. Bring to a boil and cook until tender but not falling apart, 10 to 15 minutes. Drain in a colander, rinse with cold water, and let cool. Slice into ½-inch rounds and place in a large serving bowl.

Cook the bacon in a large skillet over medium heat, about 10 minutes, until crisp. Remove to a plate lined with paper towels and let cool. Using your hands, crumble the bacon and set aside. Drain off all of the bacon fat except for about 2 tablespoons, add the onions and thyme to the pan, and cook until the onions are translucent, about 5 minutes.

To make the dressing: In a small bowl, whisk together the vinegar, olive oil, mustard, sugar, and salt and pepper to taste.

Combine the bacon and onions with the potatoes. Add the dressing and parsley and toss gently to combine. Season again with salt and pepper. Keep refrigerated until ready to serve.

SERVES 6

Cajun Potato Salad

Some basic recipes may seem easy but they're never done quite right. Potato salad is one, and my sister-in-law, Alyssa, has it down pat. It's not too mayonnaisey, not too mustardy, not too mushy. One of her secrets is Tony Chachere's Seasoning, a staple Cajun spice blend in every Louisiana household and now available throughout the United States. Although it's not absolutely essential (if you skip it, add a dash of cayenne and more salt to taste in its place), it's worth searching out.

2½ pounds large red potatoes

3 large eggs

2 kosher dill pickles, diced

½ red onion, chopped

¼ cup mayonnaise

¼ cup plus 2 tablespoons Dijon mustard

1 teaspoon freshly ground black pepper

½ teaspoon kosher salt

1 teaspoon Tony Chachere's Original Creole Seasoning (optional)

Wash the potatoes and cut into quarters. Put in a large pot, cover with cold water, and bring to a boil. Cook for 10 to 15 minutes, or until the potatoes are tender when pierced with a knife, but not mushy. Drain. Peel the skin off of most of the potatoes, leaving a bit on if you want a more homemade look. Chop into bite-sized (about ½-inch) pieces, and let cool completely.

To hard-boil the eggs, place in a medium pot of cold water and bring to a boil. Remove from the heat, cover, and let sit for 15 to 20 minutes. Drain carefully and let cool before shelling them. Chop into small pieces.

In a large bowl, stir together the potatoes, eggs, pickles, and onion. Add the mayonnaise, mustard, pepper, salt, and the Tony Chachere's Seasoning, if using. Chill for 1 hour before serving.

SERVES 4 TO 6

Cold Soba Noodles and Snap Peas with Sesame Dressing

Japanese soba noodles are made with buckwheat and have a delicate nutty taste. Because they aren't as starchy as regular wheat noodles, they don't stick together, and they make a lovely, light salad. This salad is versatile and could be made with anything from sliced cucumber and hard-boiled egg to boiled, peeled shrimp. Pre-toasted sesame seeds are available at most Asian grocery stores. Toast your own by placing sesame seeds in a dry skillet over low heat and stirring until fragrant and light brown. Remove immediately to a plate to cool.

DRESSING

¼ cup unseasoned rice vinegar

3 tablespoons soy sauce

1½ tablespoons sugar

1 teaspoon sesame oil

½ teaspoon salt

12 ounces soba noodles

1 small red bell pepper cut into 2-inch matchsticks

¼ pound snap peas, trimmed and destringed

1 carrot, cut into 2-inch matchsticks

2 tablespoons toasted sesame seeds

To make the dressing: Whisk together all of the ingredients in a small bowl. Set aside.

Add the soba noodles to a large pot of boiling water. When it reaches a boil again, add 1 cup cold water. Bring to a boil again and add 1 cup cold water again. Cook until just tender, 3 to 5 minutes. Drain in a colander and rinse with cold water.

Combine the soba in a large bowl with the bell pepper, snap peas, and carrot. Toss gently with the dressing and sprinkle with the sesame seeds.

SERVES 4

Roasted Chicken Salad with Red Grapes and Pecans

Full of sweet grapes and crunchy pecans, the salad speaks for itself, but makes a great sandwich, too. Although it calls to roast your own chicken breasts, it's perfectly fine to use leftover roast chicken from a previous dinner or roast chicken purchased at a supermarket, either dark or white meat. A dressing made with half mayonnaise and half plain yogurt keeps it from being too heavy.

4 sprigs fresh rosemary

2½ pounds boneless chicken breasts, skin on

1 tablespoon extra-virgin olive oil

1½ cups pecan halves (about 6 ounces)

2 cups small red seedless grapes, halved

2 stalks celery halved lengthwise and cut into slices (about 1 cup)

½ cup roughly chopped tender celery leaves from the heart

⅓ cup chopped red onion

¾ cup mayonnaise

¾ cup plain whole milk yogurt

1 tablespoon freshly squeezed lemon juice

Kosher salt

Freshly ground black pepper

Preheat the oven to 400°F. Take 2 of the rosemary sprigs and tuck a little bit beneath the skin of each chicken breast. Rub the olive oil on the bottom of a roasting pan, place the remaining 2 rosemary sprigs in the pan, and place the chicken breasts on top, skin up. Roast the chicken until cooked through, 30 to 40 minutes. Let cool completely. Remove the skin and rosemary from the chicken and chop the chicken into ¼-inch pieces. Place in a large bowl.

Add the pecan halves to a small, dry skillet over medium heat. Toast, stirring and turning, until fragrant, about 3 minutes. Remove to a plate and let cool. Roughly chop the pecans and set aside.

Remove the leaves from the stems of the cooked rosemary. Chop finely and add to the chicken. Add the grapes, pecans, celery, celery leaves, and onion.

In a separate large bowl, combine the mayonnaise, yogurt, and lemon juice. Season to taste with salt and pepper. Combine the dressing with the chicken mixture, tossing gently. Season again with salt and pepper. Cover and refrigerate until ready to serve.

SERVES 6

MAIN COURSES

EVEN IN THE DEAD OF WINTER, THE SMELL OF HAMBURGERS on the grill is enough to evoke the memory of a summer picnic. Few would say no to a burger, but for an upscale event thread shrimp onto skewers to make colorful kabobs, or try Vietnamese-style grilled beef dipped into a lime and black pepper sauce. And for those who haven't mastered the briquet, there's no grilling necessary for salmon paired with a cumin-scented raita or Spanish-style potato omelet sliced into wedges. Now, get cooking and enjoy.

Cold Slow-Roasted Salmon with Cucumber-Cumin Raita

Summertime on the West Coast is wild King salmon season and the time to enjoy this beauty of a fish in every way possible. Slow-roasting is one of the best ways to go: it keeps the flesh moist and delicate without losing flavor to a poaching liquid. This recipe is for a whole side of salmon, but you can use the same directions as a guide for any size fillet. Served with tangy Indian raita, this elegant picnic fare deserves a cold bottle of champagne. When transporting the salmon, make sure to keep it chilled until it's ready to eat. The raita can be kept in a separate container and spooned alongside.

1 filleted side of salmon, skin on, 2 to 3 pounds (about 1½ inches thick in the center), pinbones removed

2 tablespoons extra-virgin olive oil

Kosher salt

Freshly ground black pepper

RAITA

2 teaspoons cumin seeds

2 English cucumbers, peeled and diced

1 teaspoon kosher salt

2 cups plain whole milk yogurt

1 tablespoon freshly squeezed lemon juice

2 teaspoons finely chopped garlic

Sprinkle of cayenne pepper

Preheat the oven to 275°F. Rub both sides of the salmon with the olive oil. Place salmon skin-side down in a roasting pan. Generously sprinkle salt and pepper over the flesh side. Roast uncovered 25 to 35 minutes. The salmon will look undercooked on the top, but if it flakes when gently pulled apart with a fork, it's done. Remove and serve at room temperature.

To make the Raita: Place the cumin seeds in a large dry skillet over medium heat. Stir for 2 minutes until fragrant. Remove to a plate and cool. Place in a spice grinder or clean coffee grinder and grind well. In a medium bowl, combine the cucumbers and the salt; mix well and let sit for 15 to 30 minutes, then drain any accumulated liquid. Add the ground cumin seeds, yogurt, lemon juice, and garlic, and mix to combine. Sprinkle the top with the cayenne. Let sit for 10 minutes. Chill until ready to serve.

SERVES 4 TO 6

Spanish-Style Tortilla with Potatoes and Spinach

This recipe is similar to a traditional Spanish tortilla, a thin omelet made with potatoes. The potatoes are poached in olive oil, then drained of the remaining oil, making them silken smooth and rich in taste. The omelet keeps well and is good the next day, too. Using prewashed and packaged spinach shaves off a lot of the prep time. If you don't have a cast-iron skillet, make sure you use a skillet that can stand the heat of a broiler.

1 cup olive oil

1 pound large red potatoes, peeled and cut into ¼-inch rounds

1½ cups chopped onion (1 large)

2½ teaspoons kosher salt

8 ounces stemmed spinach leaves

7 large eggs

¼ teaspoon freshly ground black pepper

Heat the olive oil in a 10-inch cast-iron skillet over medium heat. Add the potatoes, onion, and 1 teaspoon of the salt, stirring and turning occasionally, until the potatoes are tender but not browned, 15 to 20 minutes. Drain the potatoes in a colander set over a bowl, reserving the olive oil. Let cool.

In a large pot of lightly salted boiling water, add the spinach and cook for 30 seconds, or until the spinach is wilted. Drain in a colander and run under cold water to stop the cooking. Drain again and using your hands, squeeze hard to extract the water from the spinach as best as you can and roughly chop.

Lightly beat the eggs in a large bowl, then stir in the spinach, the remaining 1½ teaspoons salt, and the pepper. Add 1 tablespoon of the reserved olive oil to the skillet over medium heat. Fan the potatoes out to cover the bottom of the pan and add the egg and spinach mixture. Cook over low heat, covered, until the sides are set but the center is still loose, about 12 minutes. Preheat the broiler.

Remove from the heat, uncover, and place the tortilla on the top rack directly under the broiler for about 2 minutes, or until golden brown. Remove from the oven and let cool for about 15 minutes. Using a spatula, gently loosen the sides and slide the tortilla onto a plate. Wait until serving time to slice.

SERVES 6 TO 8

Grilled Shrimp, Zucchini, and Tomato Skewers

Grilling shrimp in their shells keeps them succulent and moist. Prepare these skewers before you go on your picnic and cook them on site. Just make sure to not let them sit in the marinade for too long; the acid in the lemon juice can actually begin to "cook" the shrimp.

MARINADE

1 cup finely chopped fresh cilantro

½ cup extra-virgin olive oil

¼ cup freshly squeezed lemon juice

1 tablespoon finely chopped garlic

Kosher salt

Freshly ground black pepper

1 pound large shrimp, shell on

2 large zucchini, cut in half lengthwise and crosswise into 1-inch pieces

24 cherry tomatoes

To make the marinade: In a large bowl, whisk together the cilantro, olive oil, lemon juice, garlic, and salt and pepper to taste.

To devein the shrimp, using kitchen scissors, snip the shell starting at the top and follow the ridge until you almost reach the tail. Remove the vein. Leave the rest of the shell, including the legs, intact.

Add the shrimp, zucchini, and tomatoes to the marinade. Cover with plastic wrap and refrigerate for 1 hour. Place at least 12 twelve-inch bamboo skewers in cold water to soak for a couple hours (this should keep them from drying out before you reach the picnic).

Alternately thread the shrimp (twice, through the tail and upper body), tomatoes, and zucchini onto the skewers, leaving plenty of room on each skewer end to hold on to so that you can easily turn the skewer on the grill. Discard the marinade. Put skewers in a well-sealed container with ice packs to transport, making sure to keep the shrimp cool.

Prepare a grill for a hot fire. Place the shrimp over direct heat with the ends of the skewers facing away from the fire and out (to make them easier to turn), and cook until the shrimp are pink and cooked through, about 2 minutes per side. Remove from the grill and serve immediately or at room temperature.

SERVES 4

Grilled Beef Skewers with Black Pepper–Lime Dipping Sauce

A takeoff on a Vietnamese dish called "shaking beef," this dish is all about the dipping sauce, which strikes a perfect balance between salty, sour, and sweet. Bring the marinated and skewered steak with you to the picnic and grill it there. Either dip the skewered steak directly into the sauce, or eat it Vietnamese style, served with big leaves of crisp red leaf lettuce alongside to wrap the steak in and eaten like a taco. The lettuce makes for a refreshing crunch.

2 pounds filet mignon, cut into ¾-inch cubes

¼ cup minced garlic

8 teaspoons soy sauce

4 teaspoons fish sauce

4 teaspoons sugar

8 big red leaf lettuce leaves (optional)

DIPPING SAUCE

⅔ cup freshly squeezed lime juice (about 5 limes)

2 teaspoons sugar

2 teaspoons freshly ground black pepper

Kosher salt

Combine the steak with the garlic, soy sauce, fish sauce, and sugar and let marinate at room temperature for 30 minutes.

To make the Dipping Sauce: In a small container, combine the lime juice, sugar, pepper, and salt (a generous amount) and set aside.

Place eight 10-inch bamboo skewers in cold water to soak for a couple hours (this should keep them from drying out before you reach the picnic). Thread the beef, dividing it equally among the skewers. To transport, place in a well-sealed container kept cool with ice packs.

Prepare a grill for a hot fire and place the beef over direct heat with the ends of the skewers facing away from the fire and out (to make them easier to turn). Cook for 6 to 8 minutes, turning occasionally to brown on all sides. Serve immediately along with the Dipping Sauce, and lettuce, if desired.

SERVES 4 TO 6

Grilled Sausages with Sweet Roasted Pepper Relish

Nothing beats a good grilled sausage, cooked so that the hot juices pop when you take a bite. Slathered with good German mustard, it's a treat, but topped with this easy relish, it's even better. Serve the sausage in a quality bun or à la carte. The relish can be made a day in advance and will keep in the refrigerator for at least a week.

RELISH
olive oil for greasing

2 pounds (about 4 large) red and yellow bell peppers

1¼ cups chopped red onion

¼ cup water

2 tablespoons sugar

1 tablespoon white wine vinegar

1½ teaspoons kosher salt

1 teaspoon Worcestershire sauce

1 teaspoon Tabasco

6 good-quality sausages, fresh or smoked

6 good-quality sausage buns

To make the relish: Preheat the oven to 400°F. Brush a baking sheet with the olive oil. Slice the bell peppers in half through the stem end. Trim and devein, removing the seeds. Place the bell peppers cut-side down on an oiled baking sheet. Roast for 30 minutes, or until the skin on the peppers is getting slightly charred and wrinkled. Remove from the oven and place the bell peppers on a plate. Cover with a plastic bag and let steam until cool. Remove the skins and chop (you should have about 2 cups).

Combine the bell peppers and onion in a medium bowl. Add the rest of the relish ingredients and toss well to combine. Makes 2 cups. Cover and chill for at least 4 hours.

Prepare a grill for a hot fire. Place the sausages over direct heat, turning every few minutes for about 10 minutes. Depending on the type and size of the sausage, the time will vary. (Smoked sausages are already cooked and only need to be grilled long enough to give them a smoky flavor and to heat them all the way through.)

Serve the sausages in buns toasted on the grill, with a generous spoonful of the relish and any other condiments of your choice.

SERVES 6

Spicy Turkey Burgers with Tequila

Mashed avocado and sliced ripe tomatoes are essential fixings for these plump, juicy turkey burgers. The Sweet Roasted Pepper Relish (page 67) would also make a great accompaniment. For a picnic that involves transportation, make the patties ahead of time; until they're ready to grill, keep them stored in an airtight, leakproof container inside a cooler with ice packs. Beware that the heat of chiles varies greatly. The best thing to do is taste them before you mix them into the meat, adding more or less accordingly.

2 pounds ground dark meat turkey

1 cup minced onion

3 tablespoons dried bread crumbs

2 tablespoons tequila

2 tablespoons extra-virgin olive oil

1 tablespoon minced garlic

2 to 3 teaspoons minced fresh serrano chiles

2 teaspoons minced fresh oregano

2 teaspoons kosher salt

½ teaspoon ground cumin

½ teaspoon ground coriander

8 good-quality buns

Combine all the ingredients in a large bowl and, using your hands, mix well, but gently. Chill for at least 20 minutes. Form into 8 patties.

Prepare a grill for a medium-hot fire. Place the patties over direct heat and cook 4 to 6 minutes per side, or until cooked through. Serve at once on buns, with fixings such as avocado, tomato, red onion, and fresh cilantro.

SERVES 8

DIVINE DESSERTS

THERE ARE TWO KINDS OF PICNIC DESSERTS: THOSE THAT CAN be thrown into a backpack for a hike (think Ultimate Chocolate Chip–Oatmeal Cookies, Brown Sugar Blondies with Pecans, and Lemon and Crème Fraîche Loaf Cake) and those that call for a bit more delicate handling, such as a Nectarine Tart. But with the exception of the English Berry Summer Pudding (which is just so good and easy the recipe had to go in), everything here is finger fare. Toss the forks, and get rid of the spoons. If food tastes better when it's eaten outdoors, it tastes even better when it's eaten with your hands.

Moist Chocolate Walnut Cake

Pit some fancy chocolate confection against this quick and humble recipe, and I guarantee, this cake will win everyone's favor. The oatmeal adds a mild, undetectable sweetness, and the brown sugar and melted chocolate chips make it moist and impossible to put down.

1¾ cups boiling water

1 cup rolled oats

1 cup brown sugar

1 cup granulated sugar

1 stick (8 tablespoons) unsalted butter at room temperature

2 large eggs, beaten

1 teaspoon vanilla extract

1¾ cups all-purpose flour

1 tablespoon cocoa powder

1 teaspoon baking soda

1 teaspoon salt

One 12-ounce package chocolate chips

¾ cup chopped walnuts (about 4 ounces)

Preheat the oven to 350°F. Grease and flour a 9-by-13-inch cake pan.

In a large bowl, pour the boiling water over the rolled oats. Let stand for 10 minutes. Add the brown sugar, granulated sugar, and butter and stir until the butter melts. Add the eggs and vanilla and combine.

In another large bowl, sift together the flour, cocoa, baking soda, and salt. Add to the oatmeal mixture and stir until combined. Add half of the chocolate chips. Pour the batter into the pan and sprinkle the remaining chocolate chips and the walnuts on top. Bake for 40 minutes, or until a toothpick inserted into the cake (a part without a chocolate chip) comes out clean. To transport, leave the cake in the pan, wrap well with plastic wrap, and slice and serve at the picnic.

SERVES 10 TO 12

Lemon and Crème Fraîche Loaf Cake

Glazed with a tart lemon syrup, this delicate lemon cake, based on a recipe from *Desserts* by Pierre Hermé, begs for a dollop of whipped cream mixed with a bit of crème fraîche and some sliced fresh strawberries.

2⅔ cups all-purpose flour

¾ teaspoon baking powder

½ teaspoon kosher salt

2 cups sugar

6 large eggs at room temperature

Zest of 3 lemons, minced

1 vanilla bean (optional)

¾ cup crème fraîche or sour cream

3 tablespoons freshly squeezed lemon juice

1 stick (8 tablespoons) unsalted butter, melted and cooled

LEMON SYRUP

½ cup sugar

¼ cup plus 2 tablespoons water

¼ cup plus 2 tablespoons freshly squeezed lemon juice

Preheat the oven to 350°F. Grease the bottom and sides of two 9-by-5-by-3-inch loaf pans.

In a medium bowl, stir together the flour, baking powder, and salt.

In a large bowl, combine the sugar, eggs, and lemon zest. Beat the egg mixture until light and fluffy. If using a vanilla bean, use a paring knife to split the vanilla bean lengthwise and scrape the seeds into the batter. Beat briefly to blend. Stir in the crème fraîche and lemon juice and mix well. Stir in the butter.

Gradually, add the flour mixture to the egg mixture, beating just until blended. Pour the batter into the prepared loaf pans. Bake for 45 to 50 minutes, or until a toothpick inserted into the center comes out clean.

Meanwhile, prepare the Lemon Syrup: Combine the sugar, water, and lemon juice in a small pan over medium heat and stir until the sugar is totally dissolved. Set aside to cool. When the cakes are done, remove from the oven and using a skewer, make deep holes all over the top of the cakes and slowly pour the syrup over both of them. Cool the cakes in the pans for 15 more minutes, then remove and cool on wire racks. To transport, leave the loaves whole, wrap well with plastic wrap, and slice and serve at the picnic.

SERVES 16

Nectarine Tart

This gorgeous tart needs to be made a few hours in advance. Using a technique that chef Judy Rodgers of Zuni Café in San Francisco favors, it is baked using a tart pan lined with frozen, raw dough. This eliminates having to prebake the shell and also gives the nectarines time to soften and caramelize. Although the raw tart shell can be frozen for as long as a month, the tart should be baked the same day of the picnic. For a more formal tart, arrange the nectarine slices in a spiral.

TART SHELL

1½ cups all-purpose flour, plus extra for rolling

⅛ teaspoon salt

1½ sticks (12 tablespoons) cold unsalted butter

1 to 3 tablespoons ice water

TART FILLING

6 cups (about 2½ pounds) unpeeled nectarines, halved, pitted, and cut into ½-inch-thick slices

½ cup sugar

2 tablespoons cornstarch

¼ teaspoon salt

2 teaspoons all-purpose flour

1 tablespoon unsalted butter, cubed

To make the tart shell: Combine the 1½ cups flour and salt in a large mixing bowl or food processor. Cut the butter into small pieces and work into the flour, using a pastry cutter or pulsing in the food processor. When the dough resembles a coarse meal, add the ice water, 1 tablespoon at a time, just until the dough sticks together. Pat the dough into a flattened ball, wrap with plastic wrap, and refrigerate for 15 to 30 minutes.

Remove the dough and as soon as it is pliable, roll it out on a lightly floured surface into a circle approximately ⅛ inch thick and at least 13 inches in diameter. (You may have extra dough.) Gently place the rolled dough into an 11-inch tart pan with a removable bottom so that it covers the bottom and sides completely. Patch any small holes or tears by pressing on extra pieces of rolled dough glued with a dab of ice water. To remove the dough hanging over the edges of the tart pan, use a knife or take a rolling pin and roll it over the edges.

Cover the tart shell with plastic wrap and freeze (at least 1 hour and up to a month). Do not defrost the tart shell before filling with the nectarines.

(continued)

To make the tart filling: Preheat the oven to 375°F. Arrange an oven rack on the lowest level. Place the nectarines in a large bowl. Combine the sugar, cornstarch, and salt in another bowl, and mix well. Add the sugar mixture to the nectarines and gently combine. Sprinkle the flour onto the bottom of the frozen tart shell, spreading it around to thinly cover the entire bottom. (This will help prevent a soggy bottom crust.) Put the nectarine mixture into the shell and arrange the nectarines so that as many as possible are on the bottom, rather than stacked; dot the top with the butter.

Bake the tart for approximately 1 hour, or until the crust is golden brown and the nectarines are tender and a little brown or caramelized on the edges. The long baking gives the nectarines an intense flavor and helps assure that they will not be too juicy. To transport, leave in the tart pan and wrap well with plastic wrap.

SERVES 8 TO 10

Brown Sugar Blondies with Pecans

A little more refined than your average blondie, these bars are a bit lighter in texture but equally addictive and just as easy to make. Don't skip the pecans or substitute light brown sugar for the dark; they just won't be the same.

4 large eggs at room temperature

2 cups dark brown sugar

2 teaspoons vanilla extract

½ teaspoon salt

2 sticks (16 tablespoons) unsalted butter, melted and cooled

1 cup all-purpose flour

1 cup (about 4 ounces) pecans, chopped

Preheat the oven to 350°F and grease a 9-by-13-inch baking pan.

In a medium bowl, beat the eggs until frothy. Stir in the brown sugar, vanilla, and salt and mix well. Stir in the cooled butter. Add the flour and stir until everything is just blended, then mix in the pecans.

Pour the batter into the prepared baking pan and bake for 25 to 30 minutes. Cut into 1½-by-3-inch squares while still warm.

SERVES 12

Coconut Cupcakes with Cream Cheese Frosting

Sophisticated enough to seduce even adults, these cupcakes, inspired by a recipe from Ina Garten's *The Barefoot Contessa* cookbook, go quickly.

1½ cups all-purpose flour

½ teaspoon baking powder

¼ teaspoon baking soda

¼ teaspoon salt

1½ sticks (12 tablespoons) unsalted butter at room temperature

1 cup sugar

3 large eggs at room temperature

¾ cup buttermilk

1 teaspoon vanilla extract

One 7-ounce package shredded sweetened coconut

FROSTING

4 ounces cream cheese at room temperature

½ stick (4 tablespoons) unsalted butter at room temperature

½ cup plus 2 tablespoons sifted powdered sugar

½ tablespoon freshly squeezed lemon juice

½ teaspoon vanilla extract

Preheat the oven to 325°F. Line a muffin pan with 12 paper baking cups.

In a medium bowl, combine the flour, baking powder, baking soda, and salt. In another bowl, cream the butter and sugar. Add the eggs and beat until light and fluffy. Add the buttermilk and vanilla and combine. Gradually add the flour mixture just until combined. Fold in 1¼ cups of the shredded coconut.

Using a spoon, fill each muffin cup almost full with batter. Bake for 25 minutes, or just until a toothpick inserted into the center comes out clean (take care not to overcook). When the cupcakes begin to cool, remove them from the pan and let them finish cooling on a rack.

Meanwhile, to make the frosting: Beat together the cream cheese and butter until combined. Stir in the powdered sugar, lemon juice, and vanilla to a smooth, creamy consistency. Generously frost the cooled cupcakes with the cream cheese frosting. Place the remaining shredded coconut into a shallow bowl and dip the cupcakes into it to coat. To transport the cupcakes, place in a single layer in a large, airtight plastic container.

SERVES 12

Toasted Almond Bundt Cake with Raspberries

Fresh are best, but frozen, unsweetened raspberries may be substituted in this moist cake. (Do not defrost the raspberries—carefully break any clusters of frozen raspberries apart, then fold in while partially frozen.) If desired, the cake can be frosted with a mixture of equal parts sour cream and mascarpone cheese that has been sweetened with sugar. Use a Bundt pan or a 9-inch round springform cake pan.

- 1 cup slivered almonds (about 4 ounces)
- 2 sticks (16 tablespoons) unsalted butter at room temperature
- 2 cups sugar
- 6 large eggs at room temperature
- ⅔ cup sour cream
- ¾ teaspoon vanilla extract
- ¼ teaspoon almond extract
- 1½ cups all-purpose flour
- ¾ teaspoon baking powder
- ¼ teaspoon kosher salt
- 2½ cups (12 ounces) fresh raspberries, gently washed and dried
- Powdered sugar for dusting

Heat the oven to 350°F. Grease and flour a 10-inch Bundt pan.

To toast the almonds, spread them on a baking sheet and put them into the oven for 10 to 12 minutes or until lightly browned, taking care not to let them get too brown or burn. Remove from the oven to a plate and let cool. Put into a food processor and pulse until the almonds are just finely ground.

Cream together the butter and sugar in a large bowl until light and fluffy. Add eggs, 1 at a time, beating after each until blended in. Add the sour cream, vanilla, and almond extract and mix.

In a small bowl, mix together the flour, baking powder, and salt until combined. Fold the flour mixture into the egg and butter mixture. When the flour is incorporated, fold in the almonds and then the raspberries. Pour into the Bundt pan. Bake for 75 to 90 minutes, or until a toothpick inserted into the center comes out clean. (If using individual bundt pans, as pictured opposite, start checking for doneness after 30 minutes.) Dust with powdered sugar when cool. To transport, leave the cake in the pan, wrap well with plastic wrap, and slice at the picnic; before serving, dust again with powdered sugar.

SERVES 12 TO 14

English Berry Summer Pudding

White bread soaked with the season's best fruit (typically berries and currants) may not sound exciting, but give it one bite and you'll be a believer, too. Although this pudding is normally molded and turned out, this even simpler version is scooped straight from the bowl—ideally a clear bowl, in order to show off the vibrant stain of colors (glass is ideal, but a good-quality acrylic bowl would work fine, too). Make sure to bring individual bowls to serve this in because it is topped with cream.

2 pounds fresh berries (any mix of raspberries, blackberries, strawberries, or blueberries)

½ cup sugar

¼ cup water

1 to 2 tablespoons freshly squeezed lemon juice, depending upon tartness of berries

8 to 12 slices (approximately ¼-inch-wide) good-quality, slightly stale white bread such as challah

1 pint heavy cream

If using strawberries, trim and chop into smaller pieces. Place the fruit, sugar, water, and lemon juice in a large pan and bring to a boil. Reduce to a simmer. Cook very slowly, until the sugar has dissolved and the fruit begins to get juicy, 3 to 5 minutes. Stir gently. The idea is not to cook the fruit as much as to get them to release their juices. Allow the mixture to cool.

Remove the crust from the bread. In a large serving bowl, put a layer of the fruit, then top it with a layer of bread slices, being sure the bread covers the entire surface of the fruit. Continue to layer the fruit and bread, ending with the fruit. Cover the top with plastic wrap, weigh it down with something (such as a bag of rice or beans) to help the bread absorb all of the juices, and refrigerate. The pudding is best if refrigerated for at least a day before serving.

To serve, use a large spoon to scoop the pudding into a bowl, being sure to get several layers of the bread and pour a little of the unwhipped cream around it like a moat.

SERVES 6

Ultimate Chocolate Chip–Oatmeal Cookies

Perfected by my husband, a serious chocolate chip cookie (and cookie dough) connoisseur, these cookies are both chewy and crisp. You could add chopped walnuts or pecans if you want, but a purist might take offense.

2 cups rolled oats

1½ cups all-purpose flour

1 teaspoon baking soda

¼ teaspoon ground cinnamon

2 sticks (16 tablespoons) unsalted butter at room temperature

¾ cup light brown sugar

¾ cup granulated sugar

2 large eggs at room temperature

1 teaspoon vanilla extract

½ teaspoon kosher salt

One 12-ounce package chocolate chips

Preheat the oven to 375°F.

In a medium bowl, combine the oats, flour, baking soda, and cinnamon. In another bowl, add the butter, brown sugar, granulated sugar, eggs, vanilla, and salt. Beat until creamy. Gradually add in the dry ingredients until combined. Stir in the chocolate chips.

For each cookie, spoon about 2 tablespoons of dough onto an ungreased cookie sheet, spacing them a few inches apart. Bake for 15 minutes, or until the cookies are brown around the edges. Remove to a cooling rack. Repeat until all the cookies are done. When cool, store in an airtight plastic container.

SERVES 12

REFRESHING DRINKS

TOO OFTEN, BEVERAGES ARE LAST MINUTE WHEN THEY COULD be the star. A cooler packed with icy beer and sodas is expected, but a homemade drink—virgin or spiked—is appreciated. Try lemonade with a shot of ginger or a pitcher of white wine sangria afloat with nectarines and cherries. Float a few leaves of fresh mint in each glass and stand back. When it comes to drinks, it doesn't take much to impress.

Honey-Ginger Lemonade

Honey, fresh ginger, and lemons were meant for each other and this lip-smacking lemonade is the ultimate way to show them off together. Try making it with lavender honey.

4 cups water

1½ cups honey

1 cup sugar

1 cup finely chopped fresh ginger

3 cups freshly squeezed lemon juice

Bring 2 cups of the water plus the honey, sugar, and ginger to a boil in a medium saucepan. Let simmer a couple minutes until the sugar and honey are dissolved. Remove from the heat. Let stand for 20 to 30 minutes. Strain and combine with the lemon juice in a large pitcher. Let cool completely. Add the remaining 2 cups water. The lemonade should be tart-sweet at this point. Add more water to taste or serve in a pitcher over lots of ice, taking into consideration that some of it will melt and dilute the lemonade. Chill. To transport, pour into a thermos and serve over ice at the picnic.

SERVES 8

Watermelon-Lime Agua Fresca

A staple Mexican thirst quencher, *aguas frescas*—made from sweetened fruit—come in all sorts of flavors, including tamarind and cantaloupe. This is also delicious made with puréed strawberries instead of watermelon.

6 cups chunked seedless watermelon

½ cup water

3 tablespoons sugar

¼ cup freshly squeezed lime juice

Kosher salt

Lime wedges for garnish

Place the watermelon chunks in a blender and purée. In a small pan, heat the water and add the sugar, stirring until it dissolves. Remove from the heat and cool completely. Pour the watermelon purée into a pitcher. Stir in the lime juice, a pinch of salt, and the sugar water to taste. Chill. To transport, pour into a thermos and serve over ice with a garnish of lime at the picnic.

SERVES 4

Mojitos

This famous Cuban drink (pictured right) has become a favorite of everyone's. It's best if it sits for a bit so that the mint has time to infuse. For a fun twist, try using more unusual herbs, such as lemon verbena or pineapple sage.

1 cup fresh mint leaves

¾ cup light rum

½ cup freshly squeezed lemon juice

¼ cup freshly squeezed lime juice

¼ cup sugar

1⅓ cups soda water

In the bottom of a pitcher, add the mint leaves. Crush them with the back of a spoon. Add the rum, lemon juice, lime juice, and sugar and mix together. Just before serving add the soda water. Serve over ice with a garnish of mint. To transport, chill the rum mixture and pour it into a thermos, keeping the soda water separate. Serve as directed.

SERVES 4

Shandy Beer

Popular in England, this combination of a light beer and ginger beer or sparkling lemonade (look for San Pellegrino Limonata) is refreshing and thirst-quenching.

12 ounces chilled beer, such as Hefeweizen

12 ounces sparkling lemonade, ginger beer, or ginger ale

Lemon wedges for garnish

Fill 2 tall glasses with ice and pour in half beer, half lemonade. Garnish with a squeeze of lemon. To transport, bring the beer and lemonade separately. Mix and serve at the picnic.

SERVES 2

White Wine Sangria with Cherries

Although every sangria is made with fresh chunks of fruit, not every one is made with red wine. Here white wine topped with sparkling water makes a lighter, more refreshing option. If you're not going far, try presenting it in a big old-fashioned glass jar and use a ladle to serve.

⅔ cup water

¼ cup sugar

1 lemon, halved and cut into slices

1 orange, halved and cut into slices

1 nectarine, pitted and cut into wedges

12 Bing cherries, pitted and halved

½ bottle (about 1½ cups) dry white wine

Soda water

Bring the water and sugar to a boil in a small saucepan. Reduce to a simmer and cook until the sugar is dissolved. Remove from the heat and let cool.

Place the lemon slices, orange slices, nectarine wedges, and cherries in a pitcher (preferably clear, so you can see all the fruit). Add the sugar water and the wine. Stir well and chill in the refrigerator for at least 30 minutes. When ready to serve, pour the soda water into the sangria until it's to your liking. Stir well and serve the sangria over ice. To transport, pour into a thermos and serve over ice at the picnic, adding some fruit to each glass.

SERVES 6

MENUS

FROM AN ELEGANT BRUNCH TO A POST-HIKE LUNCH,

the recipes in this book offer endless options for the ultimate picnic. Here are ten menu suggestions to get you started. Once you get going though, you'll never regress to the old hot dog/chip routine again.

LATIN BARBECUE

Avocado-Tomatillo Salsa with chips
Spicy Turkey Burgers with Tequila
Mangoes with Chile, Lemon, and Salt
Brown Sugar Blondies with Pecans
Mojitos

ELEGANT BRUNCH

French Lentils with Roasted Beets and Pancetta
Roasted Chicken Salad with Red Grapes and Pecans
Spanish-Style Tortilla with Potatoes and Spinach
English Berry Summer Pudding

VEGETARIAN SPREAD

Quick Pickled Veggies
Roasted Eggplant and Bell Pepper Sandwich with Herbed Goat Cheese
Orzo Salad with Green Olives, Tomatoes, and Feta
Toasted Almond Bundt Cake with Raspberries

ROMANTIC PICNIC

Cheese Course
Chopped Spring Salad with Asparagus and Peas
Cold Slow-Roasted Salmon with Cucumber-Cumin Raita
Lemon and Crème Fraîche Loaf Cake

ALL-AMERICAN BARBECUE

Curried Deviled Eggs
Old-Fashioned Coleslaw with Apples
Grilled Sausages with Sweet Roasted Pepper Relish
Moist Chocolate Walnut Cake
Honey-Ginger Lemonade

ASIAN GRILL

Green Beans with Almond Butter–Ginger Dressing
Cold Soba Noodles and Snap Peas with Sesame Dressing
Grilled Beef Skewers with Black Pepper–Lime Dipping Sauce

POST-HIKE LUNCH

Mixed Olives with Orange and Coriander
Spiced Pine Nuts, Pecans, and Pumpkin Seeds
Fresh Mozzarella, Tomato, and Basil Sandwich
Ultimate Chocolate Chip–Oatmeal Cookies

PLAYGROUND PARTY

Meatloaf Sandwich with Chipotle Mayonnaise
Cajun Potato Salad
Melon Skewers with Lime and Mint
Coconut Cupcakes with Cream Cheese Frosting
Watermelon-Lime Agua Fresca

BEACH COOKOUT

Quick Summertime Gazpacho
Grilled Skirt Steak Sandwich with Salsa Verde
Pan Bagnat with Tuna, Tomatoes, and Olives
German-Style Potato Salad with Bacon and Mustard
Nectarine Tart
Shandy Beer

CITY PICNIC

Quick Pickled Veggies
Mixed Olives with Orange and Coriander
Prosciutto and Melon
Crusty Focaccia with Rosemary
Cheese Course

INDEX

TABLE OF EQUIVALENTS

The exact equivalents in the following tables have been rounded for convenience.

LIQUID/DRY MEASURES

U.S.	METRIC
¼ teaspoon	1.25 milliliters
½ teaspoon	2.5 milliliters
1 teaspoon	5 milliliters
1 tablespoon (3 teaspoons)	15 milliliters
1 fluid ounce (2 tablespoons)	30 milliliters
¼ cup	60 milliliters
⅓ cup	80 milliliters
½ cup	120 milliliters
1 cup	240 milliliters
1 pint (2 cups)	480 milliliters
1 quart (4 cups, 32 ounces)	960 milliliters
1 gallon (4 quarts)	3.84 liters
1 ounce (by weight)	28 grams
1 pound	454 grams
2.2 pounds	1 kilogram

OVEN TEMPERATURE

FAHRENHEIT	CELSIUS	GAS
250	120	½
275	140	1
300	150	2
325	160	3
350	180	4
375	190	5
400	200	6
425	220	7
450	230	8
475	240	9
500	260	10

LENGTH

U.S.	METRIC
⅛ inch	3 millimeters
¼ inch	6 millimeters
½ inch	12 millimeters
1 inch	2.5 centimeters